FEB 2 0 2019

D1483045

Countries We Come From

Somalia

by Adam Markovics

Consultant: Marjorie Faulstich Orellana, PhD
Professor of Urban Schooling
University of California, Los Angeles

BEARPORT PUBLISHING

New York, New York

Credits

Cover, © Homo Cosimos/Shutterstock and asiseeit/iStock; TOC, © Julian W/Shutterstock; 4, © zanskar/iStock; 5T, © Eric Lafforgue/Alamy; 5B, © Eric Lafforgue/AGE Fotostock; 7, © UN Photo/Stuart Price/CC BY-NC-ND 4.0; 8–9, © Eric Lafforgue/AGE Fotostock; 9R, © gorsh13/iStock; 10T, © blickwinkel/Alamy; 10B, © Rennett Stowe/CC BY 4.0; 11, © Till Niermann/CC BY-SA 4.0; 12, © Mike Goldwater/Alamy; 13, © Eric Lafforgue/Alamy; 14L, © Eric Lafforgue/Alamy; 14–15, © Eric Lafforgue/Alamy; 16, © British Library Board/Bridgeman Images; 17, © Africa Collection/Alamy; 18, © ACB; 19, © Free Wind 2014/Shutterstock; 20, © Free Wind 2014/Shutterstock; 21, © dpa picture alliance archive/Alamy; 22T, © fanfo/Shutterstock; 22B, © Kyselova Inna/Shutterstock; 23, © Feisal Omar/Reuters; 24–25, © Paul Fearn/Alamy; 25R, © Allstar Picture Library/Alamy; 26, © Eric Lafforgue/Alamy; 27, © Zurijeta/Shutterstock; 28, © Robert Estall photo agency/Alamy; 28–29, © Feisal Omar; 30T, © money & coins @ ian sanders/Alamy and © Anton_Ivanov/Shutterstock; 30B, © Nazy/Flickr; 31 (T to B), © imeduard/Shutterstock, © George Philipas/Alamy, © Free Wind 2014/Shutterstock, © gorsh13/iStock, © Homo Cosmicos/Shutterstock, and © yoh4nn/iStock; 32, © Lefteris Papaulakis/Shutterstock.

Publisher: Kenn Goin
Senior Editor: Joyce Tavolacci
Creative Director: Spencer Brinker
Design: Debrah Kaiser
Photo Researcher: Thomas Persano

Library of Congress Cataloging-in-Publication Data

Names: Markovics, Adam, author.
Title: Somalia / by Adam Markovics.
Description: New York : Bearport Publishing Company, 2018. | Series: Countries we come from | Includes bibliographical references and index.
Identifiers: LCCN 2017034342 (print) | LCCN 2017035793 (ebook) | ISBN 9781684025282 (ebook) | ISBN 9781684024704 (library)
Subjects: LCSH: Somalia—Juvenile literature.
Classification: LCC DT401.5 (ebook) | LCC DT401.5 .M37 2018 (print) | DDC 967.73—dc23
LC record available at https://lccn.loc.gov/2017034342

For more information, write to Bearport Publishing Company, Inc., 45 West 21st Street, Suite 3B, New York, New York 10010. Printed in the United States of America.

10 9 8 7 6 5 4 3 2 1

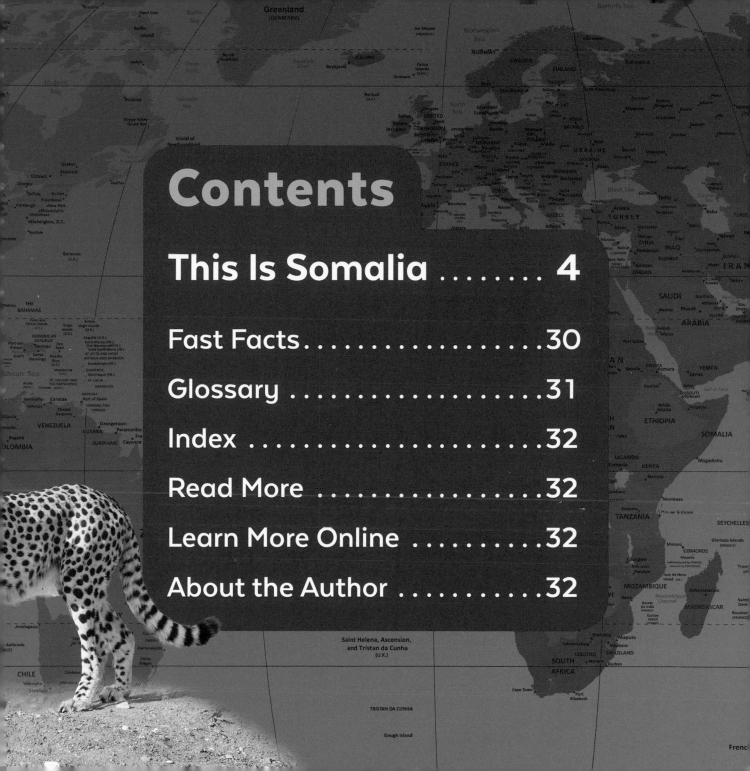

Contents

HOT

ANCIENT

Beautiful

Somalia is a country in Africa.

It has a long coastline that stretches 1,880 miles (3,025 km)!

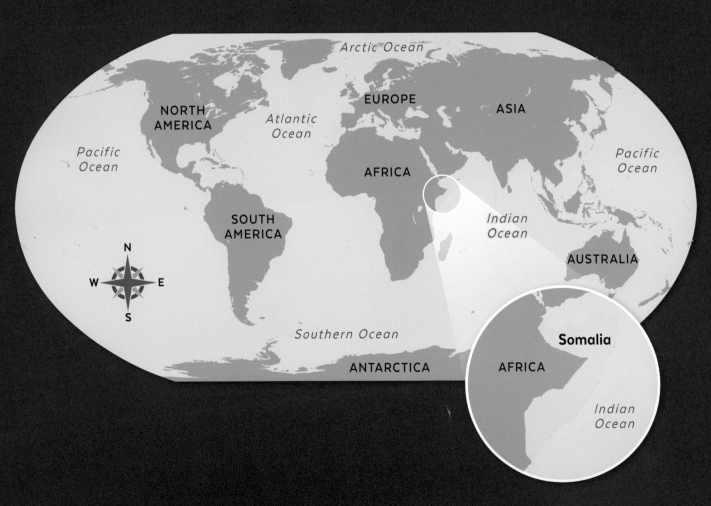

More than 13 million people live in Somalia.

Most of Somalia is hot and dry.
Rocky deserts cover much
of the land.

In the north, fewer than 4 inches (10 cm) of rain falls each year!

Drought is common in Somalia. During a drought, there's little food to eat.

Somalia is home to many kinds of animals.

Ostriches dart across the rugged land.

Antelope feed on thorny bushes.

Large groups of
furry baboons
also live in Somalia.

Many Somali people are **nomads**.

They raise camels, goats, and other livestock.

The people move with their animals from place to place.

Somali nomads live in round huts called *aqal*.

Early humans lived in Somalia thousands of years ago.

In the north, there are **ancient** cave paintings.

They are more than 5,000 years old!

Laas Geel caves

The paintings show cattle, people, and wild animals.

Over the years, England and Italy fought to rule Somalia.

Finally, in 1960, Somalia became an **independent** country.

However, Somali clans still fight to control the land.

The Somali people are split up into different clans, or families.

The **capital** of Somalia is Mogadishu.

It's also the country's largest city.

More than 1.5 million people live there.

Hargeisa is the second-largest city in Somalia.

Somali is the country's main language.

This is how you say *good morning* in Somali:

Subah wanaagsan
(soo-BAH wan-ak-SIN)

This is how you say *please*:

Fadlan
(FAD-lan)

The second most common language in Somalia is Arabic.

Somali food is full of flavor.

Meals often include rice and lamb or other meats.

Most dishes are served with a banana!

Many Somalis don't use utensils to eat. They use only their right hand.

What sports are popular in Somalia?

People love soccer.

Somalis even enjoy playing it on the beach!

Somalia is also known for its champion runners.

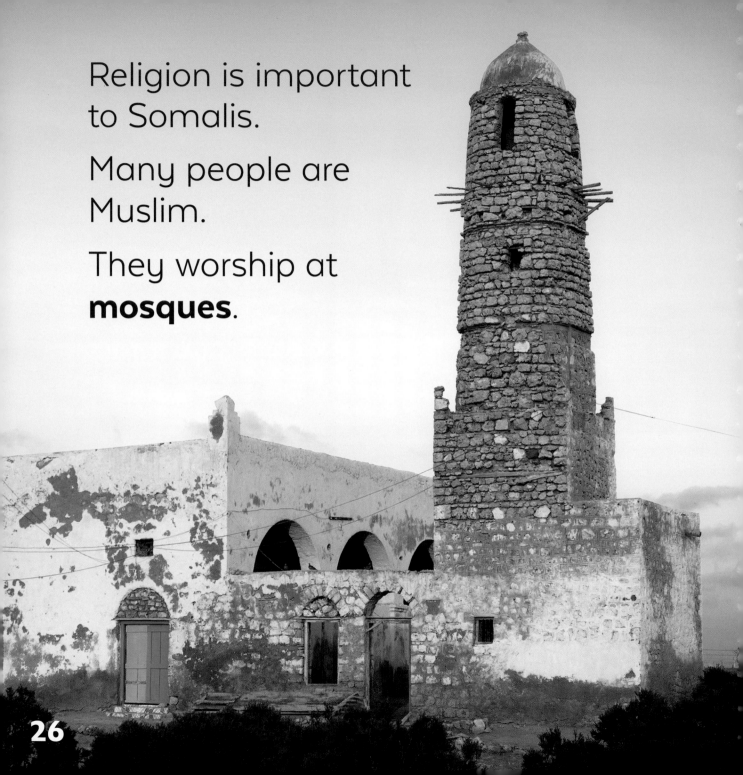

Religion is important to Somalis.

Many people are Muslim.

They worship at **mosques**.

Muslim women cover their heads with scarves.

It's time to celebrate! Somalia has many festivals.

The Istunka festival is held in the town of Afgooye.

It marks the beginning of the Somali New Year.

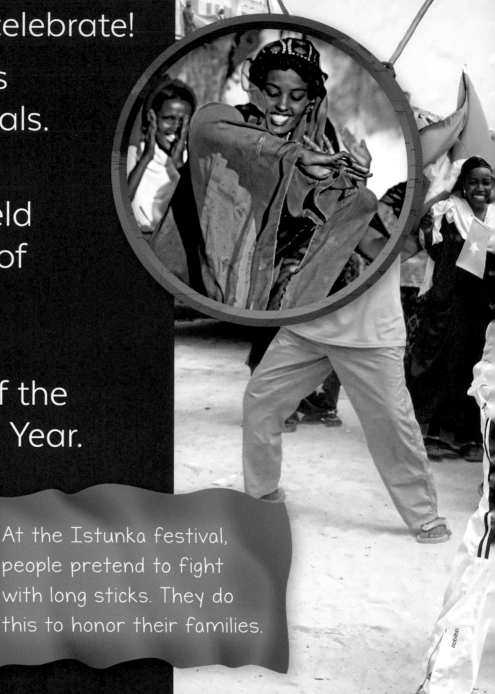

At the Istunka festival, people pretend to fight with long sticks. They do this to honor their families.

29

Fast Facts

Capital city: Mogadishu

Population of Somalia: More than 13 million

Main language: Somali

Money: Somali shilling

Major religion: Islam

Neighboring countries include: Djibouti, Ethiopia, and Kenya

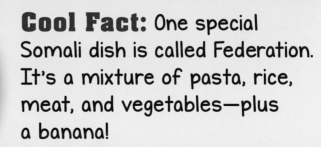

Cool Fact: One special Somali dish is called Federation. It's a mixture of pasta, rice, meat, and vegetables—plus a banana!

Glossary

ancient (AYN-shunt) very old

capital (KAP-uh-tuhl) a city where a country's government is based

drought (DROUT) a long period with little or no rain

independent (in-dee-PEN-duhnt) free of control from others

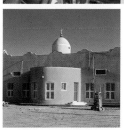

mosques (MOSKS) buildings used by Muslims for worship

nomads (NOH-mads) people who move from place to place

31

Index

Read More

Owings, Lisa. *Somalia (Exploring Countries).* Minnetonka, MN: Bellwether (2014).

Schemenauer, Elma. *Welcome to Somalia (Welcome to the World).* New York: Child's World (2008).

Learn More Online

To learn more about Somalia, visit
www.bearportpublishing.com/CountriesWeComeFrom

About the Author

Adam Markovics lives in Ossining, New York. He has a pet rabbit named Pearl who enjoys sitting next to him as he writes. He hopes to visit Africa one day soon.